HEALTH HELPERS

ALLERGIST

URSULA PANG

PowerKiDS press

Published in 2026 by The Rosen Publishing Group, Inc.
2544 Clinton Street, Buffalo, NY 14224

First Edition

Editor: Greg Roza
Book Design: Rachel Rising

Photo Credits: Cover, pp. 11, 13, 21 Pixel-Shot/Shutterstock.com; pp. 4, 6, 8, 10, 12, 14, 16, 18, 20 TechSolution/Shutterstock.com: p. 5 PeopleImages.com - Yuri A/Shutterstock.com; p. 7 Inna Vlasova/ Shutterstock.com; p. 9 YAKOBCHUK VIACHESLAV/Shutterstock.com; p. 15 Rob Byron/Shutterstock.com; p. 17 Have a nice day Photo/Shutterstock.com; p. 19 Photoroyalty/Shutterstock.com.

Names: Pang, Ursula.
Title: Allergist / Ursula Pang.
Description: Buffalo, New York : PowerKids Press, 2026. | Series: Health helpers | Includes glossary and index.
Identifiers: ISBN 9781499456431 (pbk.) | ISBN 9781499456448 (library bound) | ISBN 9781499456455 (ebook)
Subjects: LCSH: Food allergy in children–Juvenile literature. | Food allergy in children–Diagnosis–Juvenile literature. | Food allergy in children–Treatment–Juvenile literature.
Classification: LCC RJ386.5 P36 2026 | DDC 618.92975-dc23

Manufactured in China

CPSIA Compliance Information: Batch #QWPK26. For Further Information contact Rosen Publishing at 1-800-237-9932.

CONTENTS

Meet the Allergists!

Not everyone gets allergies. For those who do, however, allergies can be like having a bad cold or a bad stomachache. In some cases, allergies can be deadly. This is why we have allergists! An allergist is a health helper trained in **diagnosing** and treating all kinds of allergies.

DR. T. J

What Are Allergies?

Things that cause allergies, allergens, trick the body into thinking it's sick. Seasonal allergies are caused by things in the world around you. This could be dust, plants, pet fur, bug bites, and more. Some people are allergic to food. Food allergens include milk, nuts, bread, fish, and many other foods.

Allergy Symptoms

If you think you have an allergy, an allergist will find out. Tell them the symptoms, or signs of illness, you are having. Then they will find out what is causing them. Allergic **reactions** may include red skin, watery eyes, **sneezing**, a stomachache, and trouble breathing.

Testing for Seasonal Allergies

The allergist will give you a test to find out what exactly you are allergic to. They put different allergens on your arm or back and see which ones cause allergic reactions. This tells the allergist the best way to treat the allergic reaction.

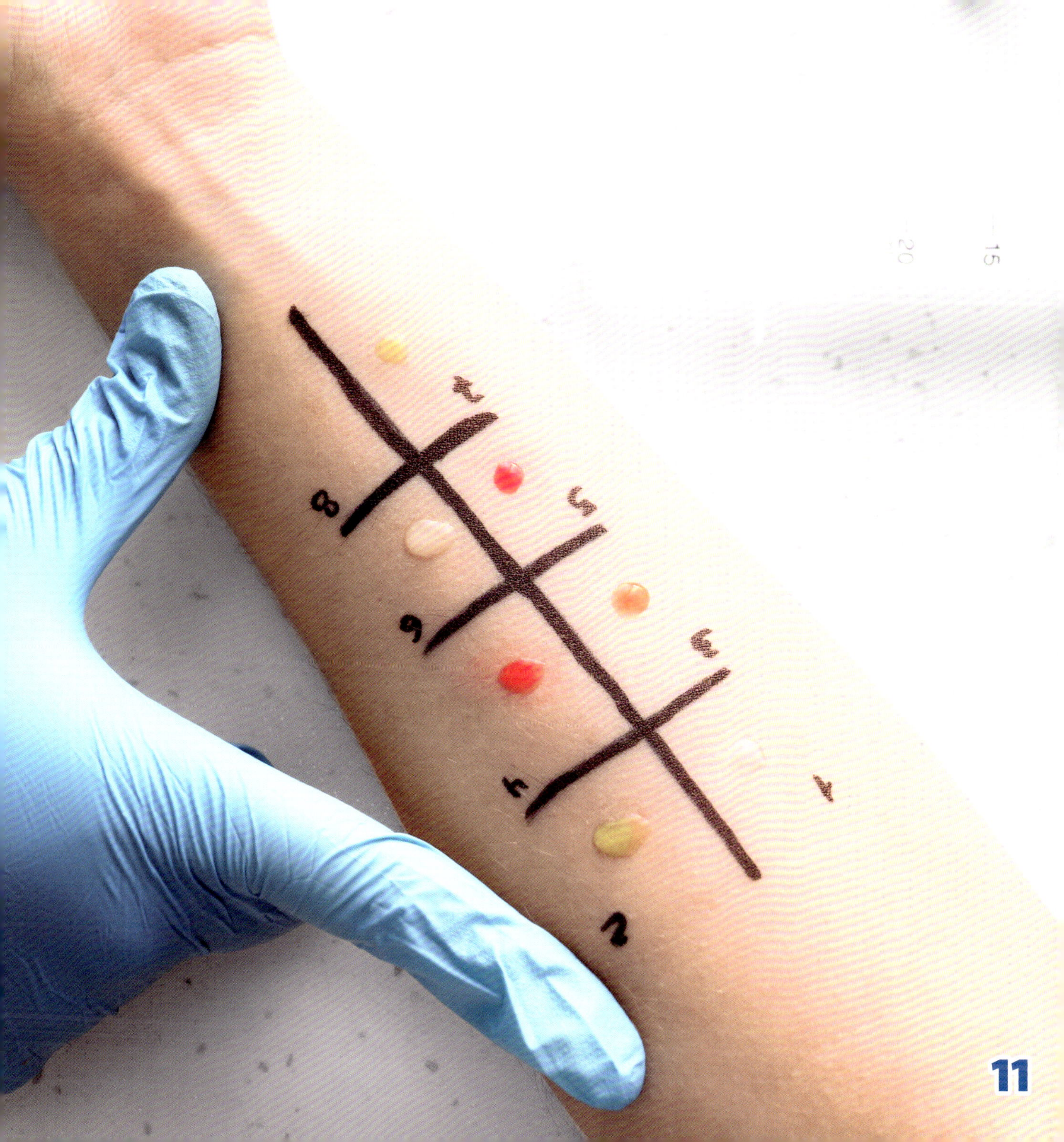

Treating Seasonal Allergies

The allergist will give you **medicine** to treat your allergy. They may give you a shot to make the signs lessen or go away. If you are having trouble breathing, they will give you a tool called an inhaler. This gives you puffs of medicine that open your airways.

inhaler

Bees and Bugs

Some people are allergic to bee **stings** and bug bites. For some, a bee sting is deadly. The allergist will give them an EpiPen. Like an inhaler, this tool puts a small amount of medicine in the body. The medicine stops the allergic reaction quickly.

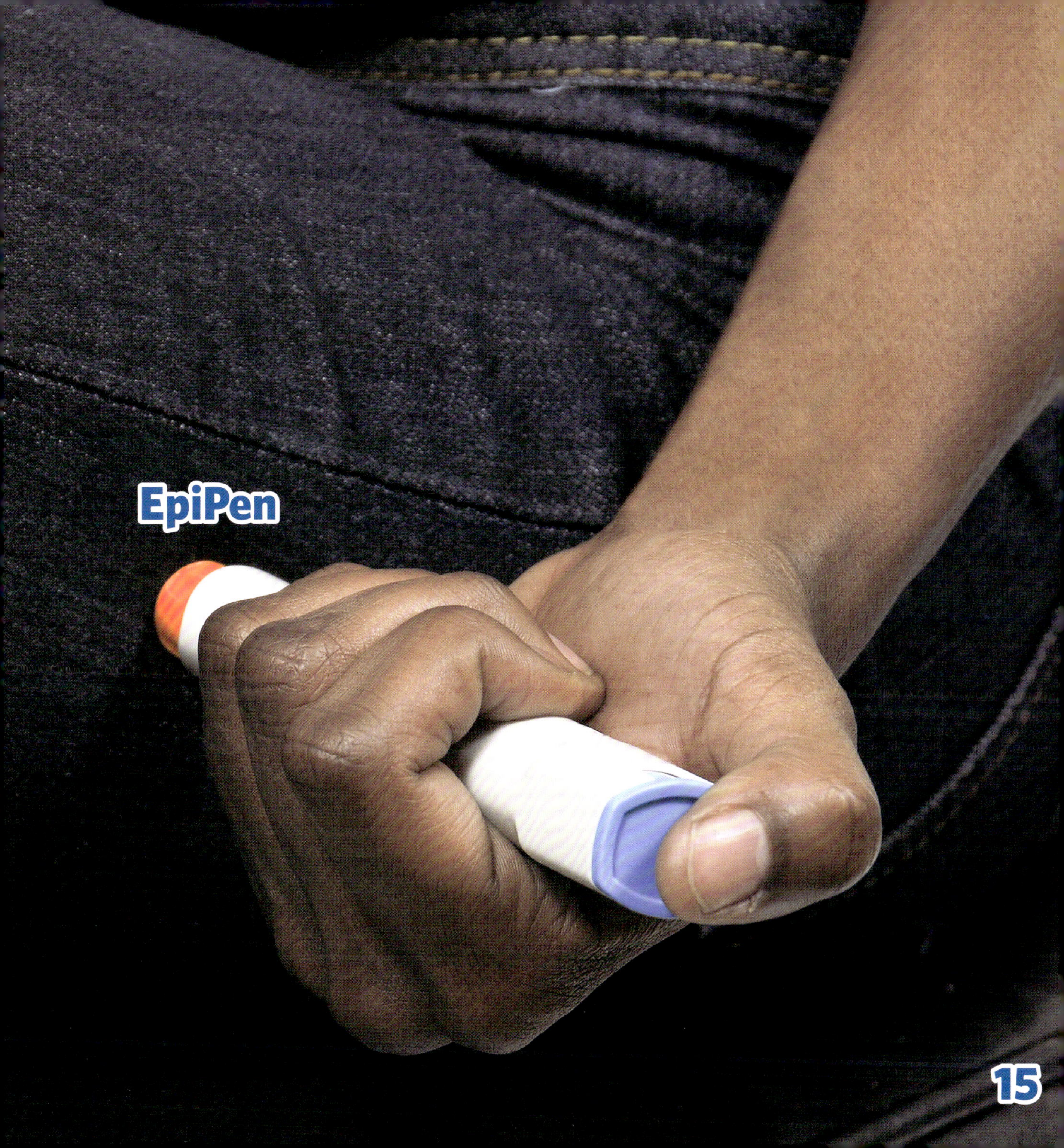
EpiPen

Testing for Food Allergies

If you think you have a food allergy, the allergist may use the same allergy test for seasonal allergies. They may look at your blood. They may give you small amounts of food until symptoms appear. This allows them to tell what foods you are allergic to.

Treating Food Allergies

Once the allergist finds your food allergen, they will tell you to **avoid** it. This is the easiest way to beat a food allergy. They will tell you to be careful when eating around others. The allergist may also give you an inhaler, EpiPen, or other medicine.

Thanks, Health Helper!

Allergists listen to you talk about your symptoms. They find out which allergens affect you, and they give you ways to avoid feeling ill. You can always go back to your allergist in the future if you need more help. Allergists care about your health!

GLOSSARY

avoid: Stay away from.

diagnose: To find and identify an illness based on symptoms, or signs.

medicine: A drug that a doctor gives you to help fight illness.

reaction: Something that happens because of something else.

sneeze: To suddenly force breath out through the nose or mouth.

sting: To prick painfully especially with a bug's stinger.

FOR MORE INFORMATION

BOOKS

Connors, Kathleen. *I Have a Bee Allergy*. Buffalo, New York: Enslow Publishing, 2023.

Wallace, Amy. *What Happens When I Have a Serious Allergy?* Buffalo, NY: PowerKids Press, 2025.

WEBSITES

Peanut Allergy
kidshealth.org/en/kids/nut-allergy.html
Find out how peanuts affect people who are allergic to them and learn how to make an emergency plan.

What Are Allergies?
kidshealth.org/en/kids/allergies.html
Read more about allergies and treatment at this informative website.

INDEX